POETRY TO PRAISE OUR GOD

Words and images to encourage your spiritual life

S. E. HARKNESS

WestBow Press books may be ordered through booksellers or by contacting:

WestBow Press
A Division of Thomas Nelson & Zondervan
1663 Liberty Drive
Bloomington, IN 47403
www.westbowpress.com
844-714-3454

Photographs by: S. E. Harkness

ISBN: 978-1-6642-9016-7 (sc)
ISBN: 978-1-6642-9015-0 (e)

Library of Congress Control Number: 2023901215

Print information available on the last page.

WestBow Press rev. date: 3/14/2023

WESTBOW
P R E S S®
A DIVISION OF THOMAS NELSON
& ZONDERVAN

Dedication

I dedicate this book to the many people who have impacted my life as a believer. There are those who have helped me along the way and I would like to say thank you to them. Moreover, I am grateful to be part of humanity, a wonderful creation by God. This world is a better place as we strived to do the best that we can to alter and set mankind on the path of goodness and righteousness.

When we dedicate ourselves to God's purpose, we impact our current lives and future generations. So, I thank God for his many blessings and further, there are three people to which I would also like to give a special thank you.

First, I am grateful to my late grandmother, Carmen. I knew you as one of the biggest givers in the family. Often times, you gave to everyone around you and was very selfless. It was your calling and purpose in life to take care of those around you and for that, I admired this quality of yours. Growing up, I saw the way you treated people and the twinkle in their eye as you walked into their home or into their place of business. I was often referred to as Carmen's granddaughter. No name, just a title. That's how much people adored you. They cared because you cared. God knew what he was doing when he placed you in the family and gifted you with such blessings that you were willing to share with all those you met. Many thanks are given to you, Gagan, the woman who freely gave and continues to give in spirit.

Second, I would like to thank my godmother, Joan. I am so blessed to have you in my life. Often times, you were like a second mother to me. You were the first person who taught me how to love myself. You worked so hard and enjoyed the best of what life had to offer. You would often so freely provide a compliment to me. I cannot tell you how much that meant to a young, quiet girl growing up in a crowded noisy city like New York. Your words were often so filled with love and positivity. It was a great light in my life. I love your goodness, your patience, your personality and all-around love of helping people. I am delighted to be your goddaughter and most importantly, your friend. Life and death are in the power of the tongue. Your words have given me power throughout my entire life and I pray that this book does the same for you.

Thirdly, thank you to my daughter, Yael. Mommy loves and adores you. You keep me happy and eager to meet a new day. My hope is that you grow into a strong young female much like all those who surround me on a daily basis. May you never lose your laughter and your joy. Love comes from the heart and the mind but also from the Word of God. Study to show thyself approve and know that through Christ anything is possible. Just believe, be good to people, hold fast to your dreams and be everything you can be in the love of Yeshua.

Last and definitely not least, to my immediate family, my mother, my father, my sisters, my nieces, and my friends. There have been many times and experiences that we have been through together. I want to say thank you for your love and help throughout the years. Life has been exceptional and I hope it will continue this way for many more years. Inspiration comes from those around us and I thank you for being my inspiration every day. I hope you feel the love that has been used in the creation of this book. I also hope it blesses you greatly. It has been a pleasure to participate in your life and help share in what you have to offer the world. I love you all and may your walk in the Lord prosper and move forward.

Preface

This book is a collection of poems for both the believer and non-believer. The religious standing of the reader is not important as long as your heart is open to the words. Many of us have something in our lives that we worship. Whether it be the Almighty God, creator of the heavens and the earth, or our spouses, our parents, our kids, our money, our work, or our popularity. Our lives are dedicated to something. This book was formed to demonstrate that above all else there is one true God, YHVH. I use the scriptures and parables (if you will) to encourage your walk as well as strengthen your faith. Furthermore, I wrote this book to help the reader experience joy, peace and mindfulness.

Some can add this poetry to their worship time. Otherwise, it can be used as a substitute for a prayer book. These words are for Christian inspiration, a break from the worldly images on our television sets, phones, and other media sources. Finally, please be inspired to receive a higher calling. As wonderful believers, we are called to be lights unto the nations. I encourage you to use these words to help you read your Bible, attend church regularly, as well as continue to spread the good news. Let this be a help to your soul.

Let me encourage the non-believers to use this book as a way to challenge their god. Look into a god that is even mightier than the god of which you serve. You may believe that this god may offer you more peace and security than the Almighty to whom we serve but, in this book, we are exploring the truth. Then, compare the gods (the one you serve and the one outlined in the text). Which one seems greater? Which one would you want fighting your battles? Which god would you like to receive gifts from? Most importantly, which god do you want to guide your life to the very end?

Contents

A morning sunrise at the beach. - original photo by S.E. Harkness

Lord, Can You Hear Me?

Silence

I would like to see you
Lord, can you hear me?

I would like to listen to you
Lord, can you hear me?

I would like to behold you
Lord, can you hear me?

I would like to worship you
Lord, can you hear me?

Breeze

I see the wind and rain
Lord, can you hear me?

I hear the birds singing
Lord, can you hear me?

I see the sky opening above
Lord, can you hear me?

I hear the valley flooding below
Lord, can you hear me?

He speaks

Lord, is that really you?
Lord, can you hear me?

I have so much to say to you
Lord, can you hear me?

This smile is for you alone
Lord, can you hear me?

Your voice is life above all
Lord, can you hear me?

He hears

I Open My Heart To You

I open my heart to you
My mind, my soul too

Each day is anew
With the glory known to few

Help me to be true
For now, and forever through

Your love is blue
The color of the never-ending ocean view

This world is only the preview
A guide for the future to-do

So, I wait for you
My eyes, my thoughts too

For a time, that is brand new
A new love that will ensue

The Heart Above All Things

The heart
It is the source of life
So perfect and right

The heart
It is the source of life
So pure and it leads us beyond the point of hope

The heart
It is the source of life
So passionate dictating our dreams

The heart
It is the source of life
So alive and beating with every step

The heart
It is the source of life
So conditional of the truth

The heart
It is the source of life
Deceitful above all things

The heart
It is the source of life
Tame it and be ye blessed

Forgiven Eve

She wandered away
She was just like us
The first of us to be exact
It was a time of purity
No sin was ever known
The earth had not known any betrayal
Innocence and purity are what had existed
And yet the serpent was more cunning than the others
I would hope that wasn't the case
Yes, it was true
It could have happened to any one of us
But it happened to her
It would be for the best of humanity
And as God would design

And so, with perfect peace
I forgive Eve
So that I may be forgiven myself
I may have done the same thing
We all may have done something similar
It was a time of confusion
And yet the time was that of triumph
It was supposed to be triumphant
But it turned out to be full of fall
I can't describe the pain, shame, and hurt
That we all felt

It was supposed to be a time of disgrace and
Then it became a time of redemption
I forgive Eve because it was a blessing
Orchestrated by God to save us all
The purpose was to redeem

It was part of the plan
Mercy was granted for her
It would have been for me too
The creation had betrayed the creator
And yet she fulfilled the plan
Helping to bring forth the Savior
Forgiveness was necessary
It will remain necessary to finish toward the end
Does forgiveness and obedience go hand in hand?
I guess it does
The more we need to obey, the more we need to forgive
Forgiveness is free to me
And given also to Eve

There You Are

There you are at a needed time
A time that will be remembered

There you are at a needed moment
A moment that was so sudden

There you are in the sky above
Lifted above the clouds for such a time as this

There you are in the eagles
They fly back and forth as if to say hello

There you are in the wind
The breath of the sky

There you are in the rain
Cooling the soil below and the temperature above

There you are in the ground beneath
I feel your love as if it were brand new

There you are in the stream near the house
Have you come to water the plants?

There you are in the trees that bear fruit
The seeds have already been replanted

There you are in my friends
Your spirit has been lifted up in their eyes

There you are in my parents
When they smile, I see your grace

There you are in church bells
The sound is reassuring

There you are in the scriptures
I love your word and the effect it has on my life

There you are in the pew
It is the sharing of the knowledge of life that is profound

There you are in the forgiveness and the salvation of many
It is the grace and the blood that allows for redemption

There you are in the people
It is the love of the Lord that provides for us all

There you are in the midst
Without you, how can we remember to be holy?

There you are in my world
Thoughts come and go, but your presence is forever

There you are in my dreams
Ever present when I wake and when I sleep

There you are in the love
A heart so full in a world so empty

There you are in the sun and the stars
The signal of that which is above

There you are in the night
Present as if to illuminate that which is in the dark

There you are below my feet
Is it you upon which I am standing?

There you are in my head
As to guide my thoughts in the right direction

There you are in my prayers
As I cry out to you, you respond right on time

There you are in my children
Your spirit moves around as though to keep life ever flowing

There you are in my ancestors
Guiding our first steps

There you are in my siblings
Whom are nourished into full trees of their own with plenty of fruit

There you are in the hairs on my head
Numbered they are, as well as nurtured

There you are in the midst of it all
Leveling and balancing that which was intended to do so

There you are in the clouds
Covering that which needs to be dimmed

There you are in the shadows
Following those you love around and around

There you are in the water
Do you nourish and fulfill?

There you are in the puddles
Gathering in groups awaiting my return

There you are above all things
Thankful am I to you

There you are in the end
I hope this time will come again

One

One thought
Is all that is needed
To turn my life around

It is the one thought
Which helps develop the potter's masterpiece
Being built from the ground

It takes one prayer
To feel the truth
And have a life brought back from the breakdown

And one hope
Which will bring that life moving forward
Good and sound

Released from the fury
The pain
Chains are loose, no longer bound

Lift up one hand
One heart
One soul to move up not down

Lift Him Up

Lift him up
And praise

Lift him up
And sing

Lift him up
And dance

Lift him up
And worship

Lift him up
And glorify

Lift him up
And magnify

Lift him up
And enjoy peace

Lift him up
And cry

Lift him up
And be saved

Lift him up
Because He is King

Prayer

Praise for which we offer up
Reverence through which we freely give
Admiration in all things that have been done
Yielding of the mind, body and spirit
Earning of the right to humbly approach
Repentance of one's sins to walk freely with God

Amen

A walk along the river. - original photo by S.E. Harkness

Down to the River

In the field, is the time she prays
A time during the day when the sun first starts to rise
She knows that she has to hurry
The morning comes and work begins

Liz runs behind the house
Further and further away into the strawberry fields
She trips on one of the numerous rocks
Which line the path down to the river

As the young girl starts to dust herself off
She begins to listen to the sounds nearby
A bird whistles, A tree whispers in the wind
The running river is crashing against the rocks

Bunnies running excitedly in the grass
Fawns follow their mother into the forest
Crushing the leaves beneath their hooves
Squirrels scurry up the tree trunk

The sounds are reassuring
Today will be a day of new beginnings
A day of cheer so full that the morning
Is extending to prolong the excitement

She brushed off her dress
It is the purple dress that grandma gave her
Liz's favorite oversized puffy purple shiny dress
That hangs low below the ankles

She examined her shoes
Brand-new straight out the box
Hiking boots with intricate and lavish details
So, everyone in the household will know that it belongs to her

This was now one of Liz's favorite outfits
The one that she wished she wore to church
It was indicative of her very essence
Beautiful, yet fun

This outfit was a blessing
And today, it was the one that would comfort her tears
She cried because of the pain in her knee
The pain from hitting it against the rock
Whilst on the walk, was unbearable

Liz opened her mouth
The words, the cries were lost
They did not come
Like a lost ship at sea, they were stranded

As she looked for the words to say
She knelt down and begin to silently pray
A prayer that her grandmother gave her
The prayer used as a comfort during times like these

Fighting back the tears, she says
Help me, Father Lord in Heaven
I was on my way down to the river
Now I have stumbled on my way

This day was supposed to be a good one
And I have hurt myself and I am in agony from the pain
I want to love this place and time
But somehow, I raise my fist at it

Help me to heal myself and the world around me
So, I will help with my love
Heal my broken wounds
And enter my heart so I can become whole

Liz stood to her feet
And she was relieved
Her stumbling, her agony
Had prompted her to pray

She did pray and things were better
She cried out and was made whole
It was a time of forthcoming bliss
Liz continued on her way down to the river

When she arrived, the pain was gone
It was appropriate now to start her chores
She knelt down to gather the water
She noticed her outfit was messy

Liz sighed and looked up
Time for another prayer
This time she immediately had the words
Her pain had subsided and now she needed to ask about her clothing

Dear Lord, if it be your will
Please help me today with my clothes
They are torn and I would like the opportunity
To wear these again on Sunday

Thank you for giving me these garments
Protect them as I go through the day
They are pleasant to the eyes and are very important to me
Everything that I have I give to you to secure

With that simple prayer
Liz accepted her torn garments
She brushed them off
Looked at her knees and cleaned them off too

She was excited
She was going to wear it one more time
Come Sunday, she would proudly display her dress and knees
For her, this was the acceptance of her answered prayers

Acceptance for the things that which she could accept
Patience to ask from God
Loving herself enough to show her imperfections
Thankful to see yet another day

Looking Up

Looking up
He notices that the clouds are unusual today
Not as full, not as glamorously fluffy
Usually, the sky is full with pictures
Or painted stories
Two gladiators that are fighting in the ring
Or maybe two sheep grazing in the field
Or better yet
Two friends running with the bulls

Each day is its own movie
A time of endless possibilities
Of images projected from the mind of God
A time of thoughts and of signs
The moon and stars sometimes appear
Yes, in the daylight with the clouds
It is a time for all the beauties of the sky
The sun, the clouds, rain, moon, and stars
How about God himself?

We remember what it means to be
A part of the universe that is created by him
There is a great world farther out
And looking up, helps us remember that
It is what makes us human
A world above our own
A simple acceptance of a greater existence than what appears
A great creator who looks down
While we are looking up

Psalms

The Psalms tell of your praises
It preaches of your compassion

Let me write a psalm of my own
One that tells of all that you have done for me

Holy is the Lord
His mercy is everlasting

When I wake in the morning
You are forever there for me

The soothing sound of the wind sings your glory
The roaring thunder speaks to your anger

The bright sunlight speaks to a warm smile
The clouds project your wonderful imagination

The rain displays your ability to water and grow all that you have planted
The stars show the twinkle in your eye

The moon speaks to your leadership and guidance through the night
The ocean is forever yours and its capacity is endless

Your beauty shows in everything you have done
They speak of your holiness, brilliance, majesty, honor, glory and mercy

Sue's Prayer

Sue wanted to pray
She wanted to pray the way the apostles did
She wanted to pray
The way, Hannah, Samuel's mother prayed

It was a deep prayer
A prayer seeking an answer, a burdensome prayer
The one where the room feels like it is spinning
A prayer in which the floor suddenly felt like quick sand

The pit of her stomach was full of remorse
The agony of the pain in her voice could be heard down the street
Sue's fingernails dug into the ground beneath
Her toenails appeared to do the same thing

Yeshua sweated drops of blood as he prayed
Sue wanted to do the same
This prayer made her back hurt and her knees bleed
As she bent over into a little ball and pushed into the floors

The prayer made her hands hurt as she clasped them together
Then pushed them into the sky to praise the Lord
Back down into the ground as to hold up her failing body
The prayer was so deep just maybe sweat, blood and tears had formed

Sue's prayer left her mouth intensely dry
She desired more than a cup of water but rather a dunk in the ocean
Her sweat accumulated then evaporated
Her neck was sore like waking after a painful night sleep

Because of her intense prayer, the blinds had seemingly crinkled
They were moving in and out from her intense breathing
The lights flickered on and off as the room shook
The floor cracked as she rocked back and forth

Her stomach pained with the emptiness of not having any food
She had fasted night and day in anticipation of the prayer
The prayer that includes blessings for her friends and family
The prayer that included the wanting of her financial improvement

She prayed for the salvation of humanity
She blessed all the believers in the world
This prayer kept her feet shaking
It also left her elbows itching

Sue left her sin chained to that floor
That intensive prayer was now complete
Sue would soon receive her answer,
Mercy for herself and all those who believed

To Him We Give The Praise

To him we give the praise
The praise worthy of a king
Lift up the hands
Lift up the feet
Lift up the voice
Honor the king
Because he is worthy
If every voice sounded like his own
No conversation would be needed
So filled with truth and love
Give thanks and praise to the Lord
Praise is important
Honor him
Give to him
Seek him
To him every praise is needed
The love that pours out of your heart
Blessings are abundant
Miracles are to follow
Sacrifices have been made
Learning his Word is golden
Giving life to his story
The final destination is heaven on earth
His people have navigated through this world
They are safe because of him
Goodness comes to those who are in need

Prayer and peace surround the loved ones
Eternity awaiting the holy remanent
Life is tolerable for those who believe
Sin is simply missing the mark
We get a new chance every day
It is love that survives during these times
Free others so that you can be freed
Above all else provide the worship
Then give him the honor
Give him the sanctification
Then give him the glory
Give him the reverence
Then give him the praise

Drip, Drop

Drip
I see the agony

Drop
I see the water

Drip
I see the blood

Drop
I see the love

Drip
I see the peace

Drop
I see the nailed hands

Drip
I see the nailed feet

Drop
I see the crown of thorns

Drip
I see the wine and gall

Drop
I see the night sky

Drip
I see the torn veil

Drop
I see the sorrow

Drip
I see the cry out

Drop
I see their laughter

Drip
I see their shouts

Drop
I see their spit

Drip
I see their strikes

Drop
I see their mocks

Drip
I see the lots

Drop
I see the clothes

Drip
I see the spirits

Drop
I see the earthquake

Drip
I see the open tombs

Drop
I see the weeping women

Drip
I see the evening

Drop
I see Joseph

Drip
I see the request

Drop
I see he is carrying you

Drip
I see the clean linen

Drop
I see the tomb

Drip
I see the stone

Drop
I see them waiting

Drip
I see the guards

Drop
I see the angels

Drip
I see the rolled away stone

Drop
I see the lying clothes

Drip
I see the angels

Drop
I see he lives

Drip
Drop

Time

In time, we are to give our life
Which is not our own

We are to use the moments
Here on earth to give to others

Our Savior spent his life and ministry
Healing the sick and preaching to the people

As his disciples, our generation is also important
We are to give to those who don't have

We are to pray for those in need
Requesting of heaven for those who want salvation

Life on earth is precious
It is sacred and it is beautiful

Giving is the key to living these moments
Praying is the key to overcoming challenges

What we do with our time benefits humanity and the planet
Embrace it and spend each moment in agreement

Keep precious memories
Close to your heart

Use it wisely
Love the time you have and the people you meet along the way

An evening sunset at the pier. - original photo by S.E. Harkness

In This Land

In this land, we are to love others like ourselves
We were indeed strangers in a foreign land

The generations we spend without our home
It is a difficult time, we are also spending without our king

It is a foreign country
An experience of knowing that which is different

But love is to turn this place around
We are to extend the love and compassion to others

A foreign love that is not the same
Trust that is not the same

We do live for a deeper purpose
One that is not so obvious

To extend God to the nations
In a time, when he is the foreigner

We were once strangers in a strange land
How do we stay afloat?

We exist to show ourselves
As the collectiveness of one God

In this strange land
Same God, same plan

The love of our God is the same for all
The differences are no challenge for him

The foreigner is a wanderer in the country
Representing different features and culture therein

And so, the resident and foreigner become one
One purpose in the love plan

Therefore, love the foreigner in the land
That the Lord thy God has given thee

It is important to the same God, that is foreign to them
He is to be one above all men

The Lord Lives

The Lord lives because he is the supreme being
He lives because he wants us to live as well
He has always existed
From the beginning to the end
From the alpha to the omega
The Lord has existed as a source of life to us all
He gave his only son as a token from the creator
His son was given as a sacrifice for the existence of others
Life is part of the Lord's nature
Existence and ever existing is part of the Lord's character
Understanding why he exists is important
Life comes from the one who is, who was and who is yet to come
Nature exists because he lives
Babies exist because he is living
Animals exist because he lived
Families exist because he is alive

If we are to be certain about all things
We must be certain about this
That he exists so that all may live
We owe him for our life and the life thereafter
His breath and hand are upon it all
Living is important to the Almighty
Naturally because it is inherent to who he is
Creation exists to have a relationship with
The creator of life

He can foster a relationship
Unlike any other
This heart is hand in hand with him who lives
The morning comes and the night falls
Because he lives
The rain falls and the sun shines
Because he lives
The babies are born and the elderly pass away
Because he lives
Before life, during our existence, and after our death
Because he lives
There is plenty of happiness and sadness
Because he lives
The beginning and the end
Because he lives
The saving and the putting away for all eternity
Because he lives
Yeshua came to the world because God wants us to dwell with him
Won't you live because he does too?

If It Is His Will

If I could define his will

His will is:
That none should perish
That I live eternally
So, I love the Lord, thy God
And
I love others
I do not sin against thee
I have love and patience
I demonstrate compassion
I feel the need to be like Yeshua
For
There is no mortality
There is no adultery
There are no false idols
There is no stealing
There is no graven images
There is no taking of the Lord's name in vain
There is no coveting
There is a reverence for the Sabbath
But
I should honor my mother and father
I feed the homeless and the fatherless
I shall love my enemies
I offer a helping hand to those in need

I will not lie and cheat
I forgive those who use me
I confess my sins
I ask for forgiveness
I accept the son
I believe in the salvation
I spend eternity with the father
Therefore
I worship
I minister to others
I forgive others
I pray without ceasing
I witness
I pray for the peace of Jerusalem
I stay alert
I work
I believe upon the Son
I am baptized
I remain fruitful
I continue the walk
I learn to love
I am transformed

Glory

Knee bending
Head bowing
Body trembling
Fingers fidgeting
Heart racing
Back breaking
Throat drying
Head lifted high above the clouds
Entering into the temple
To observe your majesty
The glory of your face is unknown to me
My face cannot observe your glory
The majesty of the creator
Is all powerful, all knowing,
My ears are focused on the sound of your voice
My fingers shake at the thought of approaching the throne
And yet I will pray without ceasing
And yet I will magnify the majesty
Till all the glory comes to you
And all the power is yours
Comfort me in your love
In your grace and I will come forth
Entering into the temple
Head lifted high above the clouds

Throat drying
Back breaking
Heart racing
Fingers fidgeting
Body trembling
Head bowing
Knee bending
In the attempt to behold your glory
The almighty God, the glorious King

Ask

Asking
What are we accepting?
The moment we begin to ask
Then do we concur with what is already in existence?
Do we put this in the universe?
Is it already there?
Asking of that which is present
Demanding that which is already alive
Or speaking it into the livelihood?
Is it now that we receive from the present?
Or do we call the future near?
Or the past long ago?
The Word tells us to ask and demand
It says that we are who we are called to be
And ask that which is placed in the mind and heart
Asking involves the speaking
Of words and our breath
To give life to that which is dead
Maybe the Word is asking us to create
This moment in which we believe
The creator created with just a word
We are called to do the same
Create with thine heart
While asking

Believe

Believing
Starts in the mind and makes its way to the heart
Also, in the heart and makes its way to the mind
Combining the two, completes the puzzle
Of bringing forth that which needs to come true
The collection of thoughts is part of the process
Necessary in the creation of our world
The heart and the mind are pushing forth the dream
Times are also important to this process
Actions are too
Tailor each moment for the end result
Focusing the mind to aim at the target
Emptying the heart to be filled with the dream
Necessary to curve the ego to remove obstacles
It is possible to open up for suggestions
Enhancing the process forthright
Those before us have counted on their visions
The vision that has been laid out before you
Numbering the steps to get there
Believing in the path of unending possibilities
They have also pleaded for the right ways
As we trust in that which is possible
The time is ripe for more believing
More blessings coming forth into present

Rightfully So

He gave his son
No greater love
That he might
Save us all

The burden of guilt
It was laid on the innocent
To set the masses free
From the sin and pain

To bury what was to be pardoned
To execute whom was to walk free
His son wanted to avoid the cross
Nails in his hands for you and me

The veil tore to unite the son, the god, and the people
He is the only way to the father
The son is the ultimate man of truth
No one without the blood stain hands approach

It was rightfully so
That he be afflicted
It was he who bore the justice
And the sins

Innocent man for the guilty
Loving for the loveless
Hurt for those who refuse to repent
Crucified for those who knew no God

He did it
For you and me
Also, Israel, the firstborn
To set them free

Rightfully so
Acceptance of God the Son
He delivered the ultimate gift
That was the greatest sacrifice

He loved us so
To give us a redeemer
His mercy extends
To the body of believers

Acceptance of the gift
Is for those who believe
It is the cross
That paved the way back to him

Blood and Water

They pierced his side
Blood and water

He could have
Cried out to be saved

The Redeemer
Was the ultimate source of life

It dripped because
Of the crucified Yeshua

He was in the rawest form
Bounded in agony

The Lord was the lamb
Slaughtered for the giving

Love and trust
Could have set him free

What was it
That made him bleed?

The piercing of his side
The burden of sin

It was the water that
Was once turned into wine

A miracle
For all to see

It was the proof before
Their eyes

The dripping
Of the two elements

Blood and water
The liquid forms of life

And evidence that
The miracle worker

Was now going
To perform

The ultimate act of
Sacrificing himself

It was necessary for life
Grace for a new beginning

Blood and water
The given gifts of life

Gift

Yeshua the gift
He embodies the giver
Clothed in majesty
He died for the opportunity
To provide life
It is so important
Once he made the crucifixion
Everyone was able to enjoy it
Most importantly
The timing was in line with the sacrifice
Appointed times were for him and us
Perfect in every way
The celebrations were upon us
It was a time for glory and sorrow
Perfect is Yeshua
Glory of the kingdom
My hope is to give back
A similar gift
For one who give the ultimate one
Worthy is the lamb that was given
Handed over to all
Given the gift that which is free
Able to love all that took part
Ultimately the gift was perfect
I have received it with love over and over again
It was made for the people and the truth therein

Above the clouds. - original photo by S.E. Harkness

In Your Name

Everything is possible
In your name

The light is forever bright
In your name

The peace that is abundant
In your name

The love that is overwhelming
In your name

Your son that died
In your name

The forgiveness
In your name

The gift of the spirit
In your name

The mountains that shake
In your name

The valleys that flood
In your name

The sun that rises
In your name

The moon that glows
In your name

The birds that sing
In your name

The people that live
In your name

The happiness that circulates
In your name

Broken chains of sin
In your name

The rocks cry out
In your name

The angels praise
In your name

Time has come and gone
In your name

The gift of salvation
In your name

Cup

A cup
For his tears
A cup for my own
It was the tears
That I didn't accept
Too much agony from the time
Within the garden
Did you know
That you were going to die?
Was your heart racing?

A cup
For his thirst
A cup for my own
It was the vinegar
That was given
Not possible to drink
Hurt more than
The piercing in your side
It was an unusual taste
One that added to your pain

A cup
For his blood
A cup for my own
How could I have saved you?
It was for me to save you
Or for you to save me, I do not know
It was a full cup that almost
Emptied my heart

A cup
For his nails
A cup for my own
Painful and above all
the source
The ultimate test of love
That pushed you
What were you thinking?
Could you sustain it
For eternity?

A cup
For your body
A cup for my own
I would drink
Of your soul
If this is what it is called
for me to do
A sinless vessel
Holds no betrayal
It holds the canvas of eternal peace

Music and Sound

Made in the image of God
Used to exalt him
Shared to portray his likeness
Included in the worship
Created for the creator

Accepted by him
Noted by the heavens
Delivered the praise

Shown above all
Overzealous in love
Upon the voices of his angels
Needed in the temple
Dedicated to his greatness

Receive (Open Hands)

Receiving
Hands out to accept more blessings
It is the creation process
The second to final step
We ask and believe
As part of the plan, we now receive
We are approached by the goodness of life
More so as creators and sometimes
As co-creators in the process
Necessary for the plan to succeed
And the blessings of prayer
They are the fruit of beginnings
Purpose wise
The blessings are the answered prayers
Our curses can be turned into our blessings
Our Savior hung from the tree
As a cursed body
Yet he was the greatest blessing
It was the love that opened the receiving
Of the gift
Almighty provides the necessities
Society receives the blessings
Humanity cultivates them into reality
He offers other blessings to be gifted
It provides that which has been given
Open thy hands and receive thy blessings

Henry Is Ready For School

Henry wakes in the morning
It is a good day
The sun is up and bursting through the window
Last night's homework had been tackled
Things had been going well
He was able to read the Bible before he went to sleep

It is time to slip out of bed
He grabs his clothes
While counting the little sheep on his shirt
He concludes there will be four opportunities
To share the gospel
Each character on his shirt indicates the day's tasks

Henry jumps in the bath
Five minutes of cleanup is all that matters
He will be renewed all day
In his heart
From his bathroom then into morning scripture reading
He read for fifteen whole minutes

Being a twelve-year old was great
It was also tough because there was a lot to do
Moment – by – moment he had to be careful
He could easily lose something
Or worst forget to do something
Better yet object to do something and suffer consciences

Henry grabs his backpack
He checks it one more time
His clothes are put together
The essay is ready to go
Time to move along
Kiss mama goodbye and off he goes to school

Henry is on his way to middle school
And he stops right before he gets on the bus
"Did I remember to pray today?"
He pondered and yet he could not remember
The thought of a missed prayer
Was extremely devastating

Henry kneeled in front of the bus
"Dear Lord, if I forgot to pray
Please forgive me, amen"
He rose, and mom was standing right behind him
"Is that your morning prayer, Henry?"
It is awfully short"

Henry knew that he didn't want to keep the bus waiting
And he should pray the complete prayer
Also, he did not want the other kids laughing at him
And of course, he wanted mama to be proud of him
"Yes Mama, I forgot and no, I am in a hurry,
Please forgive me"

"It is not my forgiveness you need
The Lord waits day and night to talk with you
He wants to follow you through the day
And he needs to hear from you
When we are in a hurry,
A quick prayer providing our thanks is all we need"

His mother was right
God sometimes wait hours to hear from us
And today he received a simple apology
The decision was between kneeling in front of friends
Or kneeling in front of God
Decisions, decisions

He dropped his bag
If it was going to be a prayer
It was going to be a big one
Knees on ground, hands in air
And tears on cheeks,
Just like grandma in front of the church on Sunday

"Dear Lord
What a wonderful God I serve
The heavens and earth sing of your goodness
You gave your only son for me
I am sorry for all the wrong that I have done
Please forgive me

Wash me in the blood of the Lord
That innocent blood that was for me
Give me the sight, the ears, the touch,
It will be for a new heart and a new mind
Help me to love like you have loved
Give as you give, in Yeshua's name, Amen"

Henry looked at mama
Then he looked at the school bus
Grandma would have been proud
He grabbed his bag
And dusted his knees
Off to school he went for a good and blessed day

Touched

Have you ever been touched
By something
You cannot explain?
It is that cold feeling
That pushes up against you
That shakes you to the core
Finally, a touch
But it is not the one
That you expected
You wanted an answered prayer
Something to get you through the day
The love of Yeshua
Comes through this touch
Sometimes when
We least expect it
That touch is the hand
Of God that holds you
That comforts you
That caress you
A young baby
Cries for his mother
She reaches out to find him
He reaches out to find her
She knows what he needs and wants
By the sound of his voice
And by his outstretched hands

God hears our cries
He searches the heart
You need him
He is there
Or he sends someone nearby?
You called out to him
He calls back
You pray to him
And he responds
With the touch on your back
Or your hand
Or your chin
Is only a reflection of
The touch that was
Already on your heart
Search him, find him,
Reach out to him
He will in turn
Search you, find you
And touch your life

In The Twilight

In the twilight
There is a sense of peace
Of the moment
When the day ends
And night begins
It is a time of rest
A time in which things take a break
A calming sleep
A chance to start again
Although the night is beginning
The evening falling
When does one get to say good night?
When the night begins
Or when the night is well underway?
When we read the Bible
It tells us that the night
Is the morning
And the day has begun already
When does the day begin?
In the evening, the nightfall
Full of void
Begins the newest of day
Out of nothing
Comes the something of the world
One may disagree with the text
But with the blank page

There is an opportunity to create
Then to behold
There is more to behold than to imagine
That is why it is said that
In the beginning, the world was full of void
With the blankness
Comes a time of new beginning
It could be a miraculous time
When we slumber, we are soon to awake
With the nightfall, the day is soon ahead
When there is blankness, then there is fullness
Embracing the twilight
Will introduce a new start

Praise

Praise is in order
To the one
Who created it all

Praise is in order
To the one
Who saves us

Praise is in order
To the one
Who grants life after death

Praise is in order
To the one
Who gave his only son

Praise is in order
To the one
Who sits on the throne

Praise is in order
To the one
Who numbers every hair

Praise is in order
To the one

Who names every star

Praise is in order
To the one
Who rules over every angel

Praise is in order
To the one
Who created all the animals

Praise is in order
To the one
Who has the eternal plan

Praise is in order
To the one
Who has sent the helper

Praise is in order
To the one
Who makes the non-existent into existence

Praise is in order
To the one
Who has been redeemed

Majesty

Your majesty
Is something to behold
The way one would if
They had received a diamond,
Bracelet, a silver plate
Or a gold jewel
The majesty of a king
Is important to his kingdom
The sheep want to know that
He is with them
Enjoying the fruit of the rulership
Such fruit is security,
Money, food, businesses, education
Is there such fruit as salvation?
Through his one and only son
The fruit nourishes all who partake
The fruit quenches all those who eat
The nourishment provided by the planter
Majesty in the sense that those
Around are in awe of his work
In awe of who he is
With the understanding of what he brings
He is above everyone
He is the majestic fruit
His majesty provides
For all that partake

Demonstrating the glory of the Father
And ultimately of the Son
And the three that become one
How often are the majesties revealed
They are given
Through the Word
And through the Spirit
The continuing of the glory
And the knowing and
Exploring of who he is
That is the majesty
The furthering of glory
And the truth for eternity
Majesty

Be Grateful

Be grateful
For all things come from him

Be grateful
It is he that provides

Be grateful
You have asked, believed and now received

Be grateful
Not all dreams go fulfilled

Be grateful
Many are called, few are chosen

Be grateful
Call out to the King of Kings

Be grateful
Acceptance of one gift can open the door to many others

Be grateful
Time is fast approaching for that glorious day

Be grateful
It is him who makes the world go around

Be grateful
Discover the goodness that is Yeshua

A day at the beach - original photo by S.E. Harkness

Peter's Call to Walk

"Peter, come forth"
He saw him in a distance
A shadow, a ghost
But how could it be?
An image walking on water
Is a sight to behold
One would not resist
A chance to receive the savior,
Or rather a rabbi, a king, a friend, or a shepherd
So many titles and yet he couldn't possibly be
A time of trial and error
A time of peace and war
A time of comfort and leave
A time to believe
Someone he could not recognize oh
I could never imagine getting this close
To walk let alone sacrifice
And yet here I am, Lord trusting in you
You that called out to Peter
You preached the same for me
A call to walk, A call to proceed
You can't even make this up
Oh, how I have to take the call
Peter took the call when he was
A fisherman on the boat
He would later answer a second call

When he was again aboard a ship
This time, to walk on water
Good ole Peter, always answering the call
Strength during the storm
It was he that was happy
To be around Yeshua once again
Walking on water is important
But most important
To do what Peter did
Answer the one who calls
While walking forward

Prayer for Salvation

Dear God
During this time
I would like to call out to you
To come into my life Lord
Save me from myself
Save me from the evil one
I love you God
I want to spend eternity with you and your son, Yeshua
He was the one to die for me
To save me from a life of pain
An eternity of endless fire
Life is not complete without the blood of Yeshua
It is not complete without the forgiveness of God
The creator and the creation are one
Without the father, there is no life
The times we live in are gloomy and bleak
So much has happened in this world
The future seems unclear
Life seems unclear
Wash me in the blood
Save me from sin
I repent
I have done wrong sometimes worthy of death
Your son Yeshua paid the price
That I may live
I want life

I need Yeshua
The Holy Spirit, I accept as my guide
Give me strength to turn away from sin
I devote myself to your word and your teachings
Helping the less fortunate is my gift to society
Preaching the gospel is my gift to you
I accept Yeshua as my personal savior
Now and forever more
Amen

Printed in the United States
by Baker & Taylor Publisher Services